ONE

DAYS

by
Pat Thomson
Illustrated by
Bob Wilson

VICTOR GOLLANCZ LTD
LONDON   1986

No, nothing like that.
I've had a very bad day.
Someone drank the goldfish water
so we were kept in after school.
Then I fell over on the way home
and I've cut my knee.

I haven't heard so much noise since your mouse escaped in the supermarket. Just wait until I tell you about all the disasters I've had today.

Go on then, Mum.
What was the first?
We'll see if your day
was as bad as mine.

It started in a small way.
I stuck my spoon in my grapefruit
and it squirted in my eye.

Then I stepped on the big broom.
The handle leaped up
and smacked me on the nose.

Squirt!!

That's quite bad
but it might have been worse.
Some people get smacked on the nose
without stepping on a broom.

I had to put cold water on my nose.
Then I combed my hair. By mistake,
I sprayed on fly spray.

Nor would anyone else.
I had to wash my hair.
Of course, the door bell rang.
I was so flustered, I shouted,
"I'm not in."
I did feel silly.

It's getting worse.
You must have felt very silly.
I'm sorry for you, really,
even if I am laughing a bit.

A Roller skate.

That's not all.
Next, Baby played outside the window.
I kept popping my head out
and calling to him.
"Boo," I said as I popped up,
and there was the window cleaner.

Yes, he did.
But he looked worried.
Then the cat got in the way
when I was tidying up.
I sucked up his tail
with the vacuum cleaner.

Don't talk to me about food.
It was no better at lunch time.
I shook the ketchup bottle
and someone had left the top loose.

Ready...steady...

Yes, and while I was cleaning up,
Baby scrambled down from the table.
He put his bowl of soup on my chair.
You can guess where I sat down.

Ready...
steady...

I was telling Mrs Oliver about it
while I was hanging the skirt out.
Then Baby slammed the door shut,
and there we were. Locked out.
I had to climb in through the window.
Everyone stood around,
giving me advice.

You win, Mum.
I had quite a good day, really.
Yours was much worse than mine.

Here we go again.

I should hope it was.
It was just one of those days.
There, I can hear Dad coming in now.
Did you remember*
to take your roller skates
out of the hall?

Ready....steady...

Wait for it!

* WHAT DO YOU THINK ?